AIRCRAFT TURBINE ENGINES
Student Workbook

SECOND EDITION

Thomas W. Wild

Production Staff

Designer/Photographer Dustin Blyer
Senior Designer/Production Manager Roberta Byerly
Editor Jeff Strong

© Copyright 2009, 2022 by
Avotek Information Resources, LLC.
All Rights Reserved

International Standard Book Number 1-933189-89-4
ISBN 13: 978-1-933189-89-5
Order # T-TURENG-0202

For Sale by: Avotek
A Select Aerospace Industries, Inc., company

Mail to:
P.O. Box 219
Weyers Cave, VA 24486
USA

Ship to:
200 Packaging Drive
Weyers Cave, VA 24486
USA

Toll Free: 800-828-6835
Telephone: 540-234-9090
Fax: 540-234-9399

Second Edition
First Printing
Printed in the USA

www.avotek.com

See our online courses at
Avotek-Online.com.

Contents

	To the Student	iv
1	History and Advancement of Turbine Engines	1
2	Turbine Principles	7
3	Terms and Engine Types	15
4	Turbine Design	21
5	Turbine Engine Systems and Maintenance	29
6	Testing and Operation	35
7	Turbofan Engines	41
8	Turboprop Engines	47
9	Turboshaft Engines and APUs	53
10	Inspection and Maintenance	59
11	Fault Analysis	67
12	Turbine Engine Manufacturing	73

To the Student

This student workbook accompanies *Aircraft Turbine Engines*, second edition, by Thomas W. Wild and John Michael Davis. This workbook should be used as a tool for highlighting the strengths and pinpointing the weaknesses of the AMT student gathering the skill and knowledge necessary to build a strong foundation in aircraft turbine engines.

The workbook was written with the assumption that the student is actively engaged in preparing for two goals: the first is to pass all required testing for the FAA Airframe and Powerplant Mechanic Certificate, and the second is to obtain the necessary skills and knowledge to function as an entry-level mechanic in the field. Both goals must be kept in mind and the material presented here has been designed to maintain that balance.

Questions on each chapter of the text are divided into three question formats and printed on perforated sheets for removal and presentation. The three types of questions are described below.

Fill in the Blank

These questions are designed to help the student understand new terminology and fundamental facts essential to understanding the chapter material.

Multiple Choice

These questions offer a broader overview of the material by offering several possible answers and allowing the student to identify the correct answer, either through recognition or through the process of elimination.

Analysis

These are complex questions that require the student to access information presented in the text, analyze the data, and record a response. Successful completion of the analysis questions shows the student has a thorough understanding of the material presented in the chapter.

The answers for the questions are available from your course instructor.

Avotek® Aircraft Maintenance Series
Introduction to Aircraft Maintenance
Aircraft Structural Maintenance
Aircraft System Maintenance
Aircraft Powerplant Maintenance

Avotek Avionics Series
Avionics: Fundamentals of Aircraft Electronics
Avionics: Beyond the AET
Avionics: Instruments and Auxiliary Systems
Avionics: Systems and Troubleshooting

Other Books by Avotek
Advanced Composites
Aircraft Corrosion Control Guide
Aircraft Hydraulics
Aircraft Structural Technician
Aircraft Turbine Engines
Aircraft Wiring and Electrical Installation
AMT Reference Handbook
Aviation Mechanic Instructor's Handbook
Avotek Aeronautical Dictionary
Fundamentals of Modern Aviation
Helicopter Maintenance
Introduction to Aircraft Structures, Systems, and Powerplants
Light Sport Aircraft Inspection Procedures
Structural Composites: Advanced Composites in Aviation
Transport Category Aircraft Systems

Chapter 1
History and Advancement of Turbine Engines

FILL IN THE BLANK QUESTIONS

name:

date:

1. The seven sections of a turbine engine, from front to back, are: __air inlet__, __compressor__, __diffuser__, __combustion chamber__, __turbine__, __exhaust__, and __accessory__.

2. Four variants (types) of turbine engines are: __turbo jet__, __turbo fan__, __turbo prop__, __turbo shaft__.

3. Newton's Laws of Motion were discovered in __1687__.

4. The earliest jet-propelled airplane was called the __He 178__.

5. __Whittle__ was granted a patent on a turbine engine in 1931.

6. Thermal barrier coatings have allowed the raising of the engine's __internal engine temp__.

7. Ultra-high-bypass engines further increase fuel economy with as much as __10%__ __(ten)__ or more of the air bypassing the core of the engine.

8. Developments in __blade cooling__ have allowed turbine inlet temperatures to be increased dramatically.

9. __additive manufacturing__ describes technologies that build up three-dimensional objects one superfine layer at a time.

Chapter 1
History and Advancement of Turbine Engines

MULTIPLE CHOICE QUESTIONS

name:

date:

1. How many types of turbine engines have been used in the aviation industry?
   a. 1
   b. 3
   c. 4
   d. 5

2. The first patent covering a turbine engine was granted to:
   a. Giovanni Branca
   b. John Barber
   c. John Bumbell
   d. Sir Thomas Boyle

3. Which German turbojet-powered aircraft was able to fly up to 500 m.p.h.?
   a. He178
   b. ME-262
   c. XP-59A
   d. Gloster Meteor

4. What was the first jet-powered aircraft to fly in America?
   a. Gloster Pioneer
   b. ME-262
   c. XP-59A
   d. XP-80

5. Jet-propelled aircraft were first built in the U.S and England by the:
   a. Whittle Company of America
   b. General Electric Corporation
   c. Bell Aircraft Corporation
   d. Hughes Aircraft Corporation

6. Engine condition monitoring ensures the overall dependability of:
   a. The engine
   b. The emissions
   c. The bearings
   d. Gas path components

7. Because wide chord blades centrifuge debris and dust into the bypass duct, they reduce the need for:
   a. Blade replacement
   b. Engine removals
   c. High clearance between blade tips and casings
   d. Temperatures increases

8. Which one of the following has reduced emissions, smoke, and fuel consumption?
   a. Improved compressors
   b. New alloys
   c. Improved combustion chambers
   d. Improved fuel distribution nozzles

9. Which development has increased the operating temperature of turbine blades by 250°C?
   a. Single crystal turbine blades
   b. Advances in laser drilling methods
   c. Wide chord blades
   d. Higher rotational speeds

10. The operation temperature at which turbine blades are able to rub against abradable shields has increased from:
    a. 1,200 to 1,800°C
    b. 350 to 1,200°F
    c. 350 to 1,200°C
    d. 350 to 1,200 K

11. Technology and systems that minimize unscheduled maintenance and eliminate premature component replacement are called:
    a. Performance analysis
    b. Real-time inlet monitoring
    c. Transient simulation
    d. Additive manufacturing

Chapter 1
History and Advancement of Turbine Engines

ANALYSIS QUESTIONS

name:

date:

1. What was Frank Whittle's contribution to the gas turbine engine's development?

2. Explain the turbine engine advancements that have led to improved fuel economy, lower emissions, reduced noise, and improved performance.

3. How are engine manufacturers improving engine efficiency?

Aircraft Turbine Engines Student Workbook | 7

Chapter 2
Turbine Principles

FILL IN THE BLANK QUESTIONS

name:

date:

1. Gases have four unique properties. They are: __pressure__, __temp__, __mass__, and __volume__.
2. A cycle consists of a/an __series of processes__.
3. The condition of a gas is determined by certain __measurable properties__.
4. Work can be accomplished by __condition__ of the gas.
5. Enthalpy is defined as __sum of the internal energy + the product of pressure__.
6. Air that does not appear to move or flow is __static__ air.
7. An additional pressure component, ram pressure in the direction of air motion, is called __total__.
8. In a subsonic convergent duct, air flow velocity will __increase__.
9. In a subsonic divergent duct, air flow velocity will __decrease__.
10. With regard to subsonic airflow through a convergent duct, pressure will __decrease__.
11. Pressure will __increase__ as subsonic air flow passes through a divergent duct.
12. The four temperature scales that are used to measure temperature are __Celsius__, __Fahrenheit__, __Kelvin__, and __Rankine temp__.
13. BTU is the abbreviation for __british thermal unit__.
14. Density is defined as __mass ÷ volume__.
15. __25__ percent of the air flowing through the combustion section of the engine is used directly for combustion.
16. The rest of the air flowing through the combustion section is used for __cooling__.
17. The symbol __Fn__ represents thrust.
18. In Newton's second law, the A stands for __Acceleration__.
19. Mass is represented by __M__ in Newton's second law.
20. The basic formula for thrust is __$\frac{W \times v_2 - v_1}{g \quad v_1}$__ $Ms = \frac{v_2 - v_1}{32.2}$

Chapter 2
Turbine Principles

MULTIPLE CHOICE QUESTIONS

name:

date:

1. A cycle consists of a series of processes. In each process the:
   a. Velocity of the fuel/air mixture remains the same
   b. Original state of the gases remains unchanged
   c. Airflow properties are changed; however, the gas returns to its original state
   d. Airflow properties are changed; however, the gas never returns to its original state

2. Work can be accomplished by changing the condition of a gas. The condition is determined by:
   a. Velocity, acceleration, temperature, and density
   b. Pressure, temperature, and volume
   c. Density, pressure, and velocity
   d. Temperature, density, and pressure

3. The molecules of a gas possess the following physical properties:
   a. Mass, momentum, energy
   b. Heat, size, momentum
   c. Weight, speed, acceleration
   d. Mass, energy, direction

4. Which principle states that when a flow of air increases in velocity, the pressure decreases?
   a. Charles' law
   b. Brayton's principle
   c. Bernoulli's principle
   d. Newton's first law

5. The changing of air pressure and velocity are affected by the shape of the duct in the engine. When it is required to convert the energy stored in the combustion gases to velocity:
   a. Divergent ducts are used
   b. Impact type turbine blades are used
   c. Convergent ducts are used
   d. Convoluted ducts are used

6. Gas turbines produce work in proportion to:
   a. The rotational speed of the engine
   b. The amount of heat produced in the engine
   c. The size of the internal ducting
   d. The amount of heat released internally

7. Heat cannot be measured directly but must be calculated from three known quantities. These are:
   a. Temperature, mass, and specific heat
   b. Specific heat, latent heat, and velocity
   c. Air density, fuel density, and mass
   d. Weight, select heat, and temperature

8. The unit defined as the amount of heat needed to increase one pound of water temperature by 1°F:
   a. British thermal unit
   b. Rankine unit
   c. Kelvin degree
   d. Specific heat unit

9. Using standard atmospheric conditions, the standard sea-level temperature is:
   a. 29°F
   b. 59°F
   c. 29°C
   d. 59°C

10. Temperature gradients in the engine can cause:
    a. Excessive pressure loss
    b. Thermal fatigue and warping
    c. No change in the engine
    d. Compounded and accelerated pressure gains

Chapter 2
Turbine Principles

MULTIPLE CHOICE QUESTIONS

name:

date:

11. Newton's First Law of Motion, generally termed the Law of Inertia, states:
    a. To every action there is an equal and opposite reaction.
    b. Force is proportional to the product of mass and acceleration.
    c. A body persists in its state of rest, or of motion in a straight line, unless acted on by some outside force.
    d. The total mass of a body is the sum of the particle accelerations and the density.

12. Density is defined as an object's:
    a. Mass times its weight
    b. Weight divided by its mass
    c. Mass divided by its volume
    d. Mass times its volume

13. Of the air that passes through an engine, what percentage is used for combustion?
    a. 100 percent
    b. 75 percent
    c. 25 percent
    d. 33 percent

14. The Brayton cycle is known as the constant:
    a. Pressure cycle
    b. Temperature cycle
    c. Mass cycle
    d. Constant cycle

15. At what stage in a turbine engine are gas pressures the greatest?
    a. Compressor inlet
    b. Turbine outlet
    c. Compressor outlet
    d. Diffuser

16. The highest gas pressure occurs at what point in an axial-flow turbofan engine?
    a. Immediately after the turbine section
    b. At the turbine entrance
    c. At the compressor outlet (diffuser)
    d. At the midpoint of the turbine

17. Gross thrust is the:
    a. Total thrust minus temperature change
    b. Total thrust when the engine is moving through the air
    c. Total thrust plus engine speed
    d. Amount of thrust generated when the engine is not moving through the air

18. Converting thrust to horsepower:
    a. Is a product of thrust and airspeed
    b. It is not possible to make a direct comparison
    c. Is the result of adding airspeed to r.p.m.
    d. Is the sum of all the velocities, divided by the altitude of the aircraft

19. Propulsive efficiency can be defined as:
    a. The amount of thrust developed by the jet nozzle compared to the energy supplied to the nozzle
    b. The product of the mass of air passing through the engine divided by the jet velocity at the nozzle
    c. How efficiently the engine extracts energy from the gas path
    d. The product of the nozzle velocity and the air temperature

20. A turbine engine's thermal efficiency tends to improve:
    a. With heat insulation
    b. When properly cooled
    c. With airspeed because of the ram effect
    d. As the engine becomes seasoned

21. Thermal efficiency is:
    a. A measure of insulating capacity
    b. Expressed as a ratio of net work produced to the fuel energy input
    c. How well the engine ejects heat
    d. Expressed as a ratio of net work produced to the fuel quantity input

Chapter 2
Turbine Principles

ANALYSIS QUESTIONS

name:

date:

1. What is the thrust produced if 20 lbs. of air is flowing through a static engine at 120 ft. per sec. (does not account for fuel flow)?

   Note: W_a = 20 lbs. of air = "mass" flow; V_2 = 120 ft./sec. = "acceleration"; g = gravity constant acceleration = 32.2 ft./sec.; V_1 = 0 because the engine is static.

2. What is the thrust if in question 1, fuel flow is taken into account? Fuel flow is 200 lbs./hr.

3. If in the engine in questions 1 and 2, the jet nozzle or exhaust nozzle is choked. What would the thrust be if A_j is 23 sq. in. and P_j is 10 p.s.i., and P_{amb} is 8 p.s.i.?

4. Calculate the horsepower being developed if a turbine wheel is producing 150 lbs. of force at a radius of 0.5 ft. and it is rotating at 35,000 r.p.m.

Chapter 2
Turbine Principles

ANALYSIS QUESTIONS

name:

date:

5. Find the horsepower if torque is given as 1600 ft.-lbs. with an r.p.m. of 2,200. Using the K constant.

6. Calculate thrust horsepower for an aircraft producing 200 lbs. of thrust at 325 m.p.h.

7. Find the horsepower being absorbed by a turbine wheel if the temperature is 1,500°F before the turbine wheel and 1,320°F after the turbine wheel with 23 lbs./sec. of flow.

8. Find the thrust-specific fuel consumption of an engine developing 1,200 lbs. of thrust and consuming 560 lbs./hr of fuel.

9. What is the propulsive efficiency of an aircraft with a velocity of 500 ft./sec with a nozzle velocity of 1,200 ft./sec?

10. Find the thermal efficiency of a turboshaft engine consuming 400 lbs./hr of fuel and is producing 500 horsepower?

Chapter 2
Turbine Principles

ANALYSIS QUESTIONS

name:

date:

Chapter 3
Terms and Engine Types

FILL IN THE BLANK QUESTIONS

name:

date:

1. Engine stations are identified on turbine engines by _numbers_.
2. Flanges on turbine engines are identified using _letters_.
3. On a turbofan engine, the fan gas path locations are identified by using numbers from _10_ to less than _20_.
4. The station number used to describe the entrance to the fan is generally _Station 1.2_.
5. Compressor pressure ratio can be expressed as a simple formula: $CPR = \frac{P_{t3}}{P_{t2}}$.
6. EPR is a ratio that is made up of two pressures: _inlet_ and _outlet_.
7. Turbofan bypass ratio is calculated using this formula: $BPR = \frac{w_{af}}{w_{ac}}$.
8. _Rockets_ can generate thrust even if there is no other source of oxygen.
9. A jet propulsion engine that has a grill of shutters at the engine inlet is the _pulse jet engine_.
10. The basic sections of a turbine engine are: _inlet_, _compressor_, _turbine_, _exhaust_, and _exhaust combustion_.
11. In a bypass fan engine, some of the thrust is generated from the _core_, but most is from the _fan_.
12. _Turboprop_ engines have a turbine for generating power and a reduction gearbox that connects to the propeller.
13. In smaller APUs, the _torus_ directs combustion gas flow onto radial-flow turbine vanes.
14. Another name for an afterburner is the _augmenter_.

Chapter 3
Terms and Engine Types

MULTIPLE CHOICE QUESTIONS

name:

date:

1. The two main components of a centrifugal compressor are the impeller and the diffuser. The diffuser:
   a. Converts velocity into pressure
   b. Converts pressure into velocity
   c. Diverts the air stream
   d. Divides the air stream

2. The abbreviation Pt7 used in turbine engine terminology means:
   a. The total inlet pressure
   b. Pressure and temperature at station No. 7
   c. The total pressure at station No. 7
   d. The partial temperature and pressure at station No. 7

3. A specific point or location in a gas turbine engine is generally identified by:
   a. EPR
   b. Color code
   c. Station
   d. Number

4. How are flanges identified on gas turbine engines?
   a. Numbers
   b. Letters
   c. Double-digit numbers only
   d. By location

5. The bypass ratio of a turbofan engine is:
   a. The amount of air that bypasses the combustion section
   b. The total mass airflow through the fan duct multiplied by the total mass airflow through the core of the engine
   c. The total mass airflow through the fan duct divided by the total mass airflow through the core of the engine
   d. The ratio of the airflow through the compressor to the airflow through the turbine

6. The types of jet propulsion engines are:
   a. Turboprop, turbojet
   b. Ramjet, pulse jet
   c. Rocket, ramjet, pulse jet, gas turbine
   d. Aft bypass, pulse jet

7. All gas turbine engines have components called the gas generator or the core. These components are:
   a. Core components 1, 2, and 3
   b. Inlet, combustor, and exhaust turbine
   c. Compressor, shaft, and turbine
   d. Compressor, burner, and turbine

8. Which of the following is not a basic gas turbine engine section?
   a. Intake
   b. Combustion
   c. Fuel control
   d. Turbine

9. An engine that ducts fan airstream through longer passages to direct the fan airstream around the outside of the core is called what?
   a. Turboprop engine
   b. Free-turbine engine
   c. Fixed-turbine engine
   d. Ducted fan engine

10. A free turbine is one that:
    a. Has no mechanical connection between the compressor and the power section
    b. Is connected directly to drive the propeller
    c. Extracts no energy from the turbine
    d. Is not speed regulated

Chapter 3
Terms and Engine Types

MULTIPLE CHOICE QUESTIONS

name:

date:

11. Turboshaft engines are commonly used as:
    a. High-torque pneumatic supply
    b. Cabin coolers
    c. Auxiliary power units
    d. Afterburners

12. Another name for an afterburner is:
    a. Auxiliary power unit
    b. Torque multiplier
    c. Exhaust booster
    d. Augmenter

1. Match the abbreviation with its definition.

Chapter 3
Terms and Engine Types

#	Abbreviation	Answer		Definition
1.	APU	G	A.	Total pressure at station No. 2
2.	EGT	I	B.	Low Pressure Compressor
3.	EPR	L	C.	Compressor pressure ratio
4.	CPR	C	D.	Vibration
5.	Fn	M	E.	High-pressure compressor
6.	HPC	E	F.	Fan speed
7.	HPT	J	G.	Auxiliary power unit
8.	LPC	B	H.	Pressure ambient
9.	LPT	P	I.	Exhaust gas temperature
10.	N_1	F	J.	High-pressure turbine
11.	N_2	O	K.	Total temperature at station No. 3
12.	P_{amb}	H	L.	Engine pressure ratio
13.	P_{s3}	N	M.	Net thrust
14.	T_{t3}	K	N.	Pressure static at station No. 3
15.	P_{t2}	A	O.	Speed of the high-pressure compressor
16.	T_{amb}	T	P.	Low-pressure turbine
17.	VIB	D	Q.	Fuel flow
18.	W_a	S	R.	Thrust specific fuel consumption
19.	W_f	Q	S.	Air flow

ANALYSIS QUESTIONS

name:

date:

Aircraft Turbine Engines Student Workbook | 21

Chapter 4
Turbine Design

FILL IN THE BLANK QUESTIONS

name:

date:

1. The type of _____material_____ used to construct parts is related to the amount of heat and load to which the parts will be subjected.

2. Compressor vanes are stationary and are placed _____after_____ a rotor section in the compressor.

3. _____abradable_____ seals are used in both compressor and turbine sections to minimize blade tip clearances or parasitic leakages in rotating seals.

4. Metal powder components are formed in dies that use _____heat_____ and _____load_____ to form the components.

5. The inlet flow should be free of _____turbulence_____ to attain maximum efficiency during operation.

6. An inlet cowl commonly used in a static test cell facility for a turbofan engine is the _____Bell mouth_____ design.

7. At high speeds, the inlet must allow the aircraft to maneuver without _____disruption airflow_____ to the compressor.

8. _____Centrifugal_____ compressors normally use only two stages because of decreased efficiencies.

9. In an axial compressor, each consecutive pair of rotor and stator blades constitutes a pressure _____stage_____.

10. Stages are numbered _____sequentially_____ from the front of the engine or the fan.

11. Most modern engines use the _____annular_____ type combustion chamber.

12. A turbine blade or vane is hollow, and cooling air flows through the blade and out through _____small holes_____ on its surface.

13. The most secure way turbine blades are retained in their groove in the turbine disk is with _____fir tree_____.

14. Most aircraft gas turbines use _____investment_____ cast turbine blades and vanes.

15. A system used to adjust the clearance between the turbine blade tips and the surrounding shroud, making them more efficient, is the _____active clearance control_____.

16. Some turbofan, turboprop, and turboshaft engines have a/an _____fixed geometry_____ convergent nozzle.

17. Gas from the engine's turbine enters the exhaust nozzle at velocities of _____750_____ to _____1,200 ft/sec_____.

Chapter 4
Turbine Design

FILL IN THE BLANK QUESTIONS

name:

date:

18. Many modern fighter aircraft that use vectored thrust incorporate a/an ___vectathrust___ type of nozzle.

19. ___acoustically absorbent linings___ are used to convert acoustic energy into heat.

20. The gear train is driven by the engine rotor through an accessory drive ___gear coupling___.

21. Turbine engines normally use ___ball___ and straight ___roller___ bearings for the main bearings.

22. A ball bearing will accept both ___thrust___ and ___radial___ loads.

Aircraft Turbine Engines Student Workbook | 23

Chapter 4
Turbine Design

MULTIPLE CHOICE QUESTIONS

name:

date:

1. What materials are used to construct the turbofan compressor system?
   a. Aluminum
   b. Titanium and nickel alloys
   c. Aluminum alloys and composites ✓
   d. Cobalt alloys

2. For a supersonic aircraft, the inlet must do what before the air reaches the compressor?
   a. Slow down the flow to subsonic speeds
   b. Remove all moisture
   c. Raise the temperature to above freezing
   d. All the above ✓

3. The purpose of a bellmouth compressor inlet is to:
   a. Provide an increased ram air effect at low airspeeds ✓
   b. Maximize the aerodynamic efficiency of the inlet
   c. Provide an increased pressure drop in the inlet
   d. Deliver the inlet air to the stator section

4. What are a compressor's primary and secondary functions?
   a. Supply combustion section air, remove all moisture,
   b. Supply user/customer bleed air, condition temperature
   c. Supply user/customer bleed air, supply combustion section with air ✓
   d. Supply combustion section air, supply user/customer bleed air

5. How does a multistage axial-flow compressor improve the efficiency of a turbine engine?
   a. More turbine wheels can be used
   b. Higher compression ratios can be obtained ✓
   c. The velocity of the air entering the combustion chamber is increased
   d. The volume of the air entering the combustion chamber is increased

6. Which two elements make up the axial flow compressor assembly?
   a. Rotor and stator
   b. Compressor and manifold
   c. Stator and diffuser ✓
   d. Diffuser and rotor

7. Between each row of rotating blades in a turbine engine compressor, there is a row of stationary blades that act to diffuse the air. These stationary blades are called:
   a. Buckets
   b. Rotors
   c. Stators ✓
   d. Airfoils

8. What is the primary factor that controls the pressure ratio of an axial-flow compressor?
   a. Number of stages in the compressor ✓
   b. Compressor inlet pressure
   c. Compressor inlet temperature
   d. Airfoil placement in the stator sections

9. What is one purpose of the stator blades in the compressor section of a turbine engine?
   a. Stabilize the pressure of the airflow ✓
   b. Control the direction of the airflow ✓
   c. Increase the velocity of the airflow
   d. Stabilize the velocity of the airflow

10. The stator vanes in an axial-flow compressor:
    a. Convert velocity energy into pressure energy
    b. Convert pressure energy into velocity energy ✓
    c. Direct air into the first stage rotor vanes at the proper angle
    d. Correct the pressure gradients in the compressor

Chapter 4
Turbine Design

MULTIPLE CHOICE QUESTIONS

name:

date:

11. An advantage of the axial-flow compressor is its:
    a. Low starting power requirements
    b. Low weight
    c. High peak efficiency
    d. Lower carbon emissions

12. An advantage of the centrifugal flow compressor is its high:
    a. Pressure rise per stage
    b. Ram efficiency
    c. Peak efficiency
    d. Peak ram effectiveness

13. A turbine engine compressor that contains vanes on both sides of the impeller is a:
    a. Double-entry centrifugal compressor
    b. Double-entry axial flow compressor
    c. Single-entry axial flow compressor
    d. Dual-exit centrifugal compressor

14. What is the primary advantage of an axial-flow compressor over a centrifugal compressor?
    a. High frontal area
    b. Less expensive
    c. Greater pressure ratio
    d. Greater thrust per thrust-specific fuel consumption

15. The diffuser section of a jet engine is between:
    a. The burner section and the turbine section
    b. Station No. 7 and station No. 8
    c. The compressor section and the burner section
    d. The inlet cowl and the compressor

16. The air passing through the combustion chamber of a turbine engine is:
    a. Used to support combustion and to cool the engine
    b. Entirely combined with fuel and burned
    c. Sped up and heated by the action of the turbines
    d. Accelerated by the combustion event

17. The turbine section of a gas turbine engine:
    a. Increases air velocity to generate thrust forces
    b. Uses heat energy to expand and accelerate the incoming gas flow
    c. Drives the compressor section
    d. Creates subsonic turbulence for noise abatement

18. What is the major function of inlet guide vanes in a turbine engine?
    a. Direct the gases in the proper direction to the tailpipe
    b. Convert a portion of the heat and pressure energy to velocity
    c. Increase the temperature of the exhaust gases
    d. Supply power to the accessory section

19. In what section of a turbojet engine is the nozzle assembly?
    a. Combustion
    b. Turbine
    c. Exhaust
    d. Compressor

20. Gill holes serve what purpose in the turbine section of a turbine engine?
    a. Cool turbine blades
    b. Propel turbine blades
    c. Reduce turbine weight
    d. Siphon off heated air for the cabin

21. What type of turbine blade is most commonly used in aircraft turbine engines?
    a. Reaction
    b. Impulse
    c. Impulse-reaction *(selected)*
    d. Impulse-retention

22. In high-bypass engines, which exhaust configuration has the core flow (gas generator) exiting the center nozzle and the fan flow exiting the fan nozzle?
    a. Fixed-geometry convergent nozzle
    b. Mixer unit noise suppressor jet
    c. Separate nozzle configuration *(selected)*
    d. Mixed nozzle configuration

23. As air flows through a divergent nozzle, the pressure of supersonic air does what?
    a. Increases *(selected)*
    b. Decreases
    c. Is inversely proportional to the temperature
    d. Is directly proportional to the temperature

24. The most intense sound at high-power engine settings comes from the:
    a. Inlet
    b. Compressor
    c. Turbine *(selected)*
    d. Exhaust nozzle

25. On turbofan engines, the gearbox or accessory section is generally mounted on the bottom front and is attached to what?
    a. Bypass fan
    b. Compressor section
    c. Combustion section
    d. Turbine section *(selected)*

26. How are bearings in a gas turbine engine identified?
    a. Numbers *(selected)*
    b. Letters
    c. Double-digit numbers only
    d. By location

27. What type of loads do ball bearings accept?
    a. Angular and perpendicular
    b. Radial and thrust *(selected)*
    c. Primary and secondary
    d. Parallel and directional

Chapter 4
Turbine Design

MULTIPLE CHOICE QUESTIONS

name:

date:

1. List and explain why certain materials are used in different areas of the engine.

2. What is the advantage of using ceramic coatings on combustion section components?

3. Explain how turbine blade and vane cooling operates.

4. Discuss the benefits of having active clearance control on a turbine engine.

Chapter 4
Turbine Design

ANALYSIS QUESTIONS

name:

date:

Chapter 5
Turbine Engine Systems and Maintenance

FILL IN THE BLANK QUESTIONS

name:

date:

1. An important property of jet fuel is its _hiss heat value_.
2. Jet A can hold contaminants in suspension because of its higher _viscosity_.
3. Microorganisms feed on the _hydrocarbons_ that are found in fuels.
4. Prist is sometimes referred to as _PFA-55MB_.
5. The engine-driven pump must be supplied with _pressurized fuel_ for the correct amount of flow at all times.
6. The three most common types of filters are _micron_, _wafer screen_, and _plain screen mesh_.
7. Hydromechanical fuel controls are mounted on the _ACC drive_ housing.
8. FCU is the abbreviation for _fuel control unit_.
9. APU fuel flow is varied in relation to the _load_ placed on the APU.
10. A permanent-magnet alternator is used to provide electric power for the _EEC_.
11. A/An _FADEC_ performs all electronic command functions necessary to operate a turbine engine.
12. Different fuel nozzle types are made, but they all generally work by spraying fuel into the combustion area under pressure through small _orifices_.
13. The turbine engine oil's _temp_ and _pressure_ are critical for the engine to run correctly and safely.
14. The _scavenge pump_ draws oil from sumps and returns it to the oil tank.
15. Ignition systems for gas turbine engines consist of _three_ main components.
16. _Automatic_ ignition systems are generally used on turboprop engines to relight the engine if it flames out.
17. All igniters, except the glow plug variety, emit a/an _sharp snapping_ noise when firing.
18. The condition when the compressor blades fail to move the air at the designed flow rate is called _compressor stall_.

Chapter 5
Turbine Engine Systems and Maintenance

FILL IN THE BLANK QUESTIONS

name:

date:

19. Two widely used types of continuous-loop heat detection systems are _Kidde_, and _fenwall_.

20. Turbine aircraft use _thrust reversers_, which work with the brakes to help slow the aircraft after landing.

Chapter 5
Turbine Engine Systems and Maintenance

MULTIPLE CHOICE QUESTIONS

name:

date:

1. Kerosene is used as turbine engine fuel because:
   a. It has very high volatility, which aids in ignition and lubrication
   b. *(circled)* It has more heat energy per gallon and lubricates fuel system components.
   c. It does not contain any water.
   d. It is readily available.

2. The primary condition that allows microorganisms to grow in the fuel in aircraft fuel tanks is:
   a. Warm temperatures and frequent fueling
   b. *(circled)* The presence of water
   c. The presence of dirt or other particulate contaminants
   d. The anaerobic conditions found in the fuel tank

3. If the engine-driven fuel pump is forced to draw fuel from the aircraft fuel system, it is said to be in suction lift. Suction lift often causes:
   a. Vapor lock
   b. Fuel foaming
   c. *(circled)* Pump cavitation
   d. Pump recirculation

4. The fuel pressure warning system:
   a. Alerts the crew when the fuel pressure is within limits
   b. Alerts the crew when the fuel pressure exceeds limits
   c. *(circled)* Alerts the crew when the fuel pressure is below the limits
   d. Alerts the crew to turn off the aux pumps

5. The speed-sensing section of an APU fuel control:
   a. *(circled)* Sets the maximum allowable speed of the engine
   b. Allows the engine to run at less than 100 percent r.p.m.
   c. Sets the bottom limit of the acceleration schedule
   d. Is used only on turbojet engines

6. In a supervisory EEC system, any fault that adversely affects engine operation causes:
   a. *(circled)* An immediate reversion to hydromechanical control
   b. The engine to go to idle thrust
   c. The engine to remain at the last power setting
   d. An immediate reversion to manual control

7. Hot spots in the combustion section of a turbojet engine are possible indicators of:
   a. Faulty igniter plugs
   b. Dirty compressor blades
   c. *(circled)* Malfunctioning fuel nozzles
   d. Excessive compressor speed

8. What is the purpose of the flow divider in a turbine engine duplex fuel nozzle?
   a. Allows an alternate flow of fuel if the primary flow clogs or is restricted
   b. *(circled)* Creates the primary and secondary fuel flows
   c. Provides a flow path for bleed air which aids in the atomization of fuel
   d. Schedules the start and run fuel patterns

9. The oil-dampened main bearing in some turbine engines is used to:
   a. Provide lubrication of bearings from the beginning of starting rotation until normal oil pressure is established
   b. *(circled)* Provide an oil film between the outer race and the bearing housing to reduce vibration tendencies in the rotor system
   c. Dampen surges in oil pressure to the bearings
   d. Provide bearing lubrication during shutdown

10. What is the purpose of the last-chance oil filters?
    a. To prevent damage to the oil spray nozzle
    b. *(circled)* To filter the oil immediately before it enters the main bearings
    c. To ensure a clean supply of oil to the lubrication system
    d. To filter the oil immediately after it leaves the main bearings

Chapter 5
Turbine Engine Systems and Maintenance

MULTIPLE CHOICE QUESTIONS

name:

date:

11. Possible failure-related ferrous metal particles in turbine engine oil cause an (electrical) indicating magnetic chip detector to indicate their presence by:
    a. Disturbing the magnetic lines of flux around the detector tip
    b. Connecting the center plug by grounding to the case
    c. Generating a small electric current that is caused by the particles being in contact with the dissimilar metal of the detector tip
    d. Activate the bridging circuit in the engine data link

12. How does the oil-to-fuel heat exchanger operate?
    a. Fuel and oil intermingle, exchange heat/cool and are separated before leaving the exchanger
    b. Fuel flows through tubes and oil is cooled as it flows around the tubes
    c. Air flows through radiator-like fins, cooling the fuel
    d. Fuel, air, and oil flow through a breather unit, exchanging heat/cool

13. The purpose of a relief valve installed in the tank venting system of a turbine engine oil tank is to:
    a. Prevent oil pressure from building up too much
    b. Maintain internal tank air pressure at the ambient atmospheric level regardless of altitude or rate of change in altitude
    c. Maintain a positive internal pressure in the oil tank after shutdown to prevent oil pump cavitations on engine start
    d. Allow the tank internal pressure to equalize too atmospheric pressure before engine shutdown

14. If a full-flow oil filter is used on an aircraft engine, and the filter becomes completely clogged, the:
    a. Oil supply to the engine is blocked
    b. Oil is bypassed back to the oil tank hopper where larger sediments and foreign matter can settle out before passage through the engine
    c. Bypass valve opens and the oil pump supplies unfiltered oil to the engine
    d. Flow of oil is reduced by half

15. The type of ignition system used on most turbine aircraft engines is:
    a. High resistance
    b. Low tension
    c. Capacitance discharge
    d. Cumulative inductive mid tension kicker circuits

16. If the r.p.m. of an axial flow compressor remains constant, the angle of attack of the rotor blades can be changed by:
    a. Changing the velocity of the airflow
    b. Changing the compressor diameter
    c. Increasing the pressure ratio
    d. Decreasing the pressure ratio

17. The purpose of a bleed valve, at the beginning stages of the compressor in an aircraft gas turbine engine, is to:
    a. Vent some of the air overboard to prevent a compressor stall
    b. Control excessively high r.p.m. to prevent a compressor stall
    c. Vent high ram air pressure overboard to prevent a compressor stall
    d. Control the bleed air being used for pressurization

18. How are most aircraft turbine engine fire extinguishing systems activated?
    a. Electrically discharged cartridges
    b. Manual remote-control valve
    c. Pushrod assembly
    d. By the detection system

1. Explain the sequence of events that take place to maintain a constant speed as a load is applied to a typical APU engine.

Chapter 5
Turbine Engine Systems and Maintenance

ANALYSIS QUESTIONS

name:

2. Explain the difference between a hydromechanical fuel control and a FADEC system using an EEC computer.

date:

3. Explain the operation of the pressure regulating oil system used on turbine engines.

4. Discuss the use of a magnetic chip detector.

Chapter 6
Testing and Operation

FILL IN THE BLANK QUESTIONS

name:

date:

1. _instrum mensuration_ is critical to monitoring the condition of the gas path.
2. A loss of oil pressure will rapidly bring on a complete _engine_ failure.
3. In the flight deck, one digital display unit can replace up to _36_ conventional analog engine gauges.
4. The _hydro mechanical torque wrench_ system uses oil pressure to measure torque.
5. Many of the aspects of operation and indication for _turbo shaft_ engines are very similar to a turboprop.
6. Operators of turbine engines must exercise _vigilance_ during the start procedure to prevent a starting problem.
7. An early indication of a hot start is a rapid rise in _fuel flow_.
8. _hung start_ occur when an engine lights off but fails to accelerate.
9. A/An _false start_ occurs when light-off fails to take place.
10. _CO_2_ is an extinguishing agent that does not contaminate the engine interior or damage any auxiliary systems.
11. Material used in constructing the _turbine section_ determines the temperature limit.
12. _Specific thrust_ is defined as the pounds of net thrust developed per pound of airflow per second.
13. Turbine engine exhaust gas temperature varies directly with turbine _inlet temp_ at a constant compression ratio.
14. During testing, _fuel_ and _oil_ samples are taken to ensure that systems are free from contamination.
15. Measured engine data must be corrected to _sea level standard day conditions_ to ensure consistent data.

Chapter 6
Testing and Operation

MULTIPLE CHOICE QUESTIONS

name:

date:

1. What is the proper starting sequence for a gas turbine engine?
   a. Ignition, starter, fuel
   b. Starter, ignition, fuel
   c. Starter, fuel, ignition
   d. Fuel, ignition, starter

2. The basic instrumentation for a turbine engine are:
   a. Tachometer, oil pressure, and fuel pressure
   b. Tachometer, oil pressure, air temperature, and burner pressure
   c. Tachometer, oil pressure, gas temperature, and fuel flow
   d. Tachometer, oil pressure, engine pressure ratio, and fuel temperature

3. In what units do turbine engine tachometers measure?
   a. Percent of engine r.p.m.
   b. Actual engine r.p.m.
   c. Percent of engine pressure ratio
   d. Percentage of power turbine r.p.m.

4. Turbine gas temperatures are which of the following?
   a. Inlet, compressor, combustor, and exhaust
   b. Exhaust gas, inter-turbine, turbine inlet, and turbine outlet
   c. Turbine gas temperature, burner inlet temperature, and compressor mid-stage
   d. Exhaust nozzle and tail cone

5. Which of the following engine variables is the most critical during turbine engine operation?
   a. Compressor inlet air temperature
   b. Compressor r.p.m.
   c. Turbine inlet temperature
   d. Ambient air pressure

6. Which of the following is used to monitor the mechanical integrity of the turbines and to check engine operating conditions of a turbine engine?
   a. Engine oil pressure
   b. Exhaust gas temperature
   c. Engine pressure ratio
   d. Multiple parameter analysis

7. Which of the following is the ultimate limiting factor of turbine engine operation?
   a. Compressor inlet air temperature
   b. Turbine inlet temperature
   c. Burner can pressure
   d. Exhaust nozzle pressure

8. Consider these two statements

   (1) Engine pressure ratio (EPR) is a ratio of the exhaust gas pressure to the engine inlet air pressure, and it indicates the thrust produced.
   (2) Engine pressure ratio (EPR) is a ratio of the exhaust gas pressure to the engine inlet air pressure, and it indicates volumetric efficiency.

   Regarding the above statements:
   a. Only No. 1 is true
   b. Only No. 2 is true
   c. Both No. 1 and No. 2 are true
   d. Neither No. 1 nor No. 2 are true

9. Torquemeters measure engine output by:
   a. Converting EGT into torque
   b. Measuring pylon deflection
   c. Using torsional deflection, hydromechanical measurements, and load cells
   d. Used only on APUs

Chapter 6
Testing and Operation

MULTIPLE CHOICE QUESTIONS

name:

date:

10. When starting a turbine engine, a hung start is indicated if the engine:
    a. Exhaust gas temperature exceeds specified limits
    b. Fails to reach idle r.p.m.
    c. R.p.m. exceeds specified operating speed
    d. Temperature and r.p.m. fluctuate and decay

11. When starting a gas turbine engine, if the EGT rises beyond the high limits, this starting problem is referred to as a:
    a. Hung start
    b. No light off
    c. Hot start
    d. Boom start

12. A flat-rated engine:
    a. Is used only on helicopters
    b. Has externally mounted cooling ducts
    c. Can exceed its power rating for a flat 3 minutes
    d. Is an engine whose power output is less than the engine's physical capacity

13. Some twin-engine aircraft have an automatic performance reserve (APR) that:
    a. Serves as a reserve of power in the event of missed approaches
    b. Allows for high density altitude performance
    c. Keeps the prop angles within limits
    d. Increases maximum thrust for one engine if the other engine loses power

14. On an aircraft turbine engine operating at a constant power, bleeding air from the compressor would result in:
    a. A noticeable decrease in compressor pressure
    b. A false compressor pressure reading on the compressor pressure gauge
    c. The engine quits running
    d. None of these answers

15. Engines that are subject to performance validation runs:
    a. Require that engine parameters be corrected for nonstandard conditions
    b. Can be performed only when standard day conditions exist
    c. Must be conducted in a no wind condition
    d. Are done only on every tenth engine

16. Why perform a cool-off period before shutting down a turbine engine?
    a. To allow the turbine wheel to cool before the case contracts around it
    b. To prevent vapor lock in the fuel control or fuel lines
    c. To prevent seizure of the engine bearings
    d. To allow the turbine wheel to assume a steady-state contraction coefficient

Chapter 6
Testing and Operation

ANALYSIS QUESTIONS

name:

date:

1. Discuss the turbofan-specific instruments that are used with turbofan engines. Include the basic operating principles.

2. Explain the basic starting sequence for starting a dual-spool turbofan engine.

3. Describe the unique instruments that are associated with a turboprop engine installation.

4. Use the chart from Figure 6-6-2 in the textbook. Determine the thrust if the outside temperature is 70°F and the pressure is 13.50 p.s.i.a.

5. Use the chart from Figure 6-6-3 in the textbook. Find the maximum ITT temperature for 60°F and a pressure of 13.9 p.s.i.a.

Chapter 6
Testing and Operation

6. Calculate the correction factors if testing an engine on a day when the temperature is 40°F and the barometric pressure is 14.49 p.s.i.a.

ANALYSIS QUESTIONS

name:

date:

Chapter 7
Turbofan Engines

FILL IN THE BLANK QUESTIONS

name:

date:

1. _turbo fan_ engines are the most efficient and economical for operating large airlines.

2. The primary _goals_ for improving gas turbine engines are to reduce fuel consumption, increase reliability and thrust, and reduce noise and exhaust emissions.

3. _Graphite_ composite used in the engine and nacelle has greatly reduced their weight.

4. Reducing the amount of bleed air from the engine's gas path for gas seals can also _reduced_ fuel consumption.

5. The Pratt & Whitney JT8D is a/an _twin_ spool _axial_ flow gas turbine engine that is equipped with a secondary air duct that encases the full length of the engine.

6. On the PW2000, electron beam welding joins the disks and spacers in the _rye_ pressure rotor.

7. Specific models of PW4000 change the last two digits to indicate the _trust_ rating.

8. The PW4000 engine is a two-spool engine and has a nominal bypass ratio of _5:1_.

9. On PW4000 series engines, the _highy_ stage air is also bled into the HPC interior to cool and stabilize the internal temperature.

10. The Rolls-Royce Trent series engine has a/an _annular_ type of combustor.

11. The CFM LEAP engine has fan blades made using a process of _resin transfer molder_.

12. Engines with a reduction gear between the fan and the rest of the rotating engine components are called _Gear turbo fan_.

Chapter 7
Turbofan Engines

MULTIPLE CHOICE QUESTIONS

name:

date:

1. Many smaller turbofan engines use a fan driven off of the:
    a. Accessory gearbox
    b. Low-speed compressor
    c. N_1 spool
    d. N_3 spool

2. Which turbine engine compressor arrangement is the most common on larger turbine engines?
    a. Dual-stage, centrifugal flow
    b. Dual-spool, axial flow
    c. Single-spool, axial flow
    d. Single-stage, dual

3. How many spools (compressors) does the typical, large turbofan engine have?
    a. 2
    b. 4
    c. 1
    d. As many as needed

4. In many turbofan engines, the N_1 rotor is supported by the:
    a. Number 5 and 6 bearings
    b. Number 2 and 4 bearings
    c. Number 1 through 6 bearings
    d. Number 1 and 2 bearings

5. The Pratt & Whitney 2000 engine uses variable stators in the first five stages of the high-pressure compressor to:
    a. Provide stability over the entire operating envelope
    b. Depress compressor efficiency during low power
    c. Provide a no-load spool down during engine shut down
    d. Allow the engine to be restarted at any flight attitude

6. What type of combustion chamber is used on the Pratt & Whitney 2000 series large turbofan engines?
    a. Can type
    b. Can-annular type
    c. Annular type
    d. Can-tubular

7. The PW4000 is a:
    a. Dual-spool turbojet
    b. Centrifugal flow turbofan
    c. High-bypass, two-spool turbofan
    d. Single-stage combined axial flow engine

8. How many stages are in the PW4000 low- and high-compressor sections?
    a. 3 stages of low and 9 stages of high
    b. 5 stages of low and 17 stages of high
    c. 5 stages of low and 11 stages of high
    d. 3 stages of low and 17 stages of high

9. The Pratt & Whitney 4000 engine has fan exit guide vanes for:
    a. Preparing the air for entry into the compressor section
    b. Straightening the discharge air before it goes into the thrust-reverser fan air duct
    c. Allowing fan air to provide engine case cooling
    d. Adding cool air thrust

10. The PW4000 combustion chamber is a:
    a. 2-piece annular design
    b. 1-piece annular design
    c. Multi can-annular design
    d. 3-piece annular design

11. The high-pressure turbine of the PW4000 contains:
    a. 1 stage
    b. 2 stages
    c. 2 stators
    d. 3 stages

Chapter 7
Turbofan Engines

MULTIPLE CHOICE QUESTIONS

name:

date:

12. The active clearance control (ACC) portion of an EEC system helps turbine engine efficiency by:
    a. Adjusting stator vane position according to operating conditions and power requirements
    b. Ensuring turbine blade to engine case clearances are kept to a minimum by controlling case temperatures
    c. Automatically adjusting engine speed to maintain a desired EPR
    d. Adjusting the clearances between the main shaft and the bearings by controlling oil temperatures

13. The 2.9 bleed valves of the PW4000 are opened by:
    a. Spring load and closed by PS3
    b. PS3 and closed by spring load
    c. PS3 and closed by 9th stage air
    d. 9th stage and closed by PS3

14. The PW4000 engine air/oil heat exchanger valve is:
    a. Always open
    b. Spring-loaded closed, and PS3 air pressure opened
    c. Open when the oil pressure difference is greater than about 60 p.s.i.d across the heat exchanger
    d. Open only when the temperature is above 400°F

15. The primary function of the HPC Secondary Flow Control system on the PW4000 is to control the flow of 9th stage cooling air to the:
    a. Secondary flow control valves
    b. Secondary flow control solenoids
    c. Aft end of the HPC inner diameter and forward side of the LPT
    d. Mid-section of the LPT

16. The PW4000 engines turbine vane and blade cooling air valves are:
    a. Open only during cruise
    b. Open only during takeoff
    c. Spring-loaded open and pneumatically closed
    d. Pneumatically opened and spring-loaded closed

17. Engines that use FADECs have a programming plug that stays with the engine. This plug contains:
    a. Engine model and serial numbers
    b. The history of the last five engine cycles
    c. Fuel flow and power settings
    d. Engine thrust rating, engine performance package, and variable stator vane schedule

18. When the oil filter becomes clogged, which one of the following occurs first?
    a. The oil filter bypass valve opens
    b. The oil filter differential pressure switch opens
    c. The oil pressure drops to zero
    d. Signal goes to EFIS

19. The ignition exciters and igniter plug cables on the PW4000 are:
    a. Not cooled
    b. Fan air cooled
    c. 13th stage air cooled
    d. Metal shielded

20. Engine oil pressure exceeding the maximum limit on the PW4000 is:
    a. An indication the fuel/oil cooler bypass valve has opened
    b. An indication the oil pressure relief valve has stuck closed
    c. Caused by operating the engine when the oil pump drive shaft has sheared
    d. Cause for engine shut down

Chapter 7
Turbofan Engines

ANALYSIS QUESTIONS

name:

date:

1. Discuss the basic gas path components that make up the primary (core) flow of the PW4000 as the airflow through the engine.

2. Explain the flow of air through the PW4000 HPC secondary airflow control system.

3. Describe the format or makeup of the FADEC system used on the PW4000.

4. Explain how information from the FADEC EEC is transmitted to output commands and how feedback information is transmitted back to the EEC.

Aircraft Turbine Engines Student Workbook | 47

Chapter 8
Turboprop Engines

FILL IN THE BLANK QUESTIONS

name:

date:

1. A __turbo prop__ uses a gas turbine to turn a reduction gear system that, in turn, drives the propeller.

2. Turboprop engines provide the __best__ specific fuel consumption of any gas turbine engine.

3. The turboprop engine has a turbine section that extracts between __75-85%__ percent of the total energy to drive the propeller.

4. Because the propeller must be driven by the __gas generator__ part of the engine, a complex propeller control system is necessary to adjust the propeller pitch for the power requirement of the engine.

5. At normal operating conditions, both the __high__ speed and __low__ speed must be coordinated to maintain the correct power setting.

6. The Pratt & Whitney PT6A engine is a turboprop, but it is also produced in a/an __turboshaft__ version that can be used as an APU.

7. The compressor turbine is separated from the power turbine by a/an __interstage__ baffle, which prevents turbine gases from transmitting heat to the turbine disk faces on the PW PT6A.

8. The difference between the oil pressure and the reduction gearbox internal oil pressure accurately indicates the __torque__ being produced by the PW PT6A.

9. Because the Honeywell TPE331 turboprop engine is a fixed turbine engine, a method of locking the propeller at approximately __zero__ pitch is needed.

10. The PW100 turboprop engine's high-pressure, single centrifugal compressor is driven by the __high__ pressure turbine.

Chapter 8
Turboprop Engines

MULTIPLE CHOICE QUESTIONS

name: Nathan

date: 02/14/24

100%

1. A turboprop powerplant propeller:
   a. Is governed at the same speed as that of the turbine
   b. Controls the speed of the engine in the beta range
   c. **Accounts for 75 to 85% of the total thrust output**
   d. Accounts for 70 to 80% of the net thrust output

2. The gas generator or gas producer of a free-turbine turboprop engine produces:
   a. Electricity
   b. Thrust
   c. **High-velocity gases that drive the power turbine**
   d. 65% of the required thrust

3. In the Pratt & Whitney PT6A engine, what is the total number of degrees of bend (turns) that the airflow undergoes from the time the air enters the engine until it exits the exhaust?
   a. **720°**
   b. 520°
   c. 360°
   d. 180°

4. What type of compressor assembly does the PT6A use?
   a. Three-stage axial
   b. Two-stage centrifugal
   c. **Three-stage axial, one-stage centrifugal (combination)**
   d. two-stage axial, two-stage centrifugal (combination)

5. How many turbines are used in the PT6A-6 (the lower horsepower version) to drive the compressor?
   a. 2
   b. 3
   c. **1**
   d. 4

6. The combustion-chamber liner in the Pratt & Whitney PT6A engine is a/an:
   a. Can type
   b. Can-annular type
   c. **Annular reverse-flow type**
   d. Can-annular reverse-flow type

7. What is the purpose of the power turbine in the PT6A?
   a. To turn the compressor
   b. To pump fuel
   c. **To drive the reduction gearbox and propeller**
   d. Provide thrust for takeoff power

8. When a negative torque signal is generated by the TPE331, the propeller:
   a. Seeks a lower blade angle
   b. Seeks a higher blade angle
   c. Moves into reverse pitch
   d. **Is automatically feathered**

Chapter 8
Turboprop Engines

ANALYSIS QUESTIONS

name:

date:

1. Draw a simple diagram of a free turbine engine, and explain the difference between a fixed and a free turbine turboprop engine.

2. Label the bearings and flanges on the diagram below.

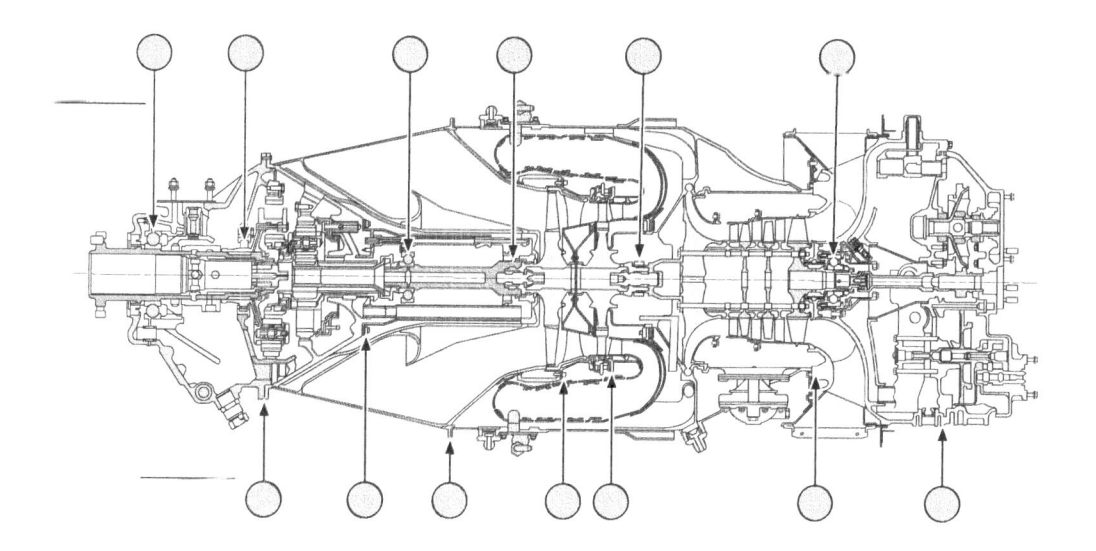

Chapter 8
Turboprop Engines

ANALYSIS QUESTIONS

name:

date:

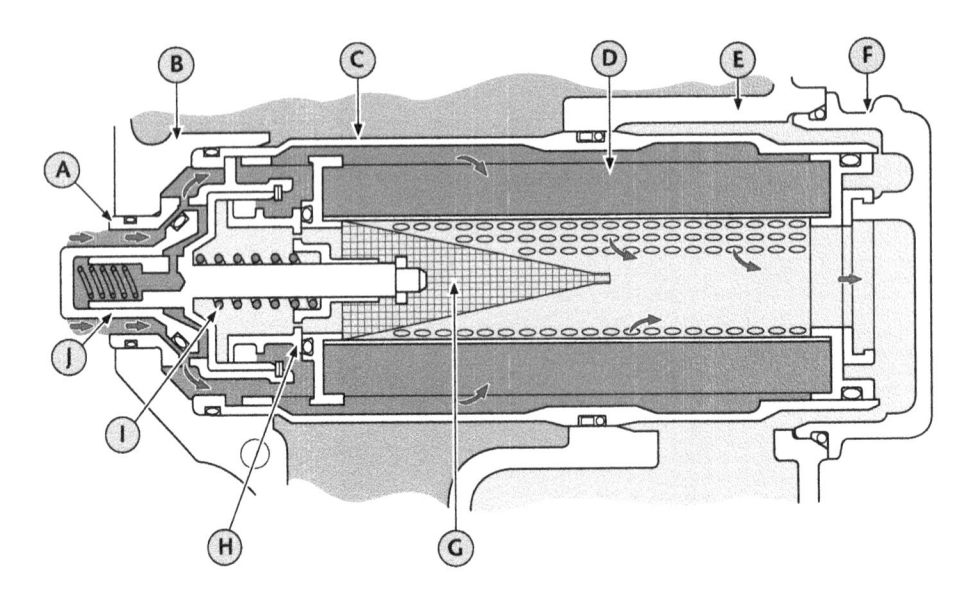

3. Label the diagram below.

A. _____

B. _____

C. _____

D. _____

E. _____

F. _____

G. _____

H. _____

I. _____

J. _____

Chapter 9
Turboshaft Engines and APUs

FILL IN THE BLANK QUESTIONS

name:

date:

1. A gas turbine engine that delivers its power through a shaft is referred to as a/an ___turbo shaft___ engine.

2. The turboshaft engine can produce some thrust but is primarily designed to produce ___shaft___ horsepower.

3. ___APU___ are designed to provide aircraft with electrical or pneumatic power to perform several on-board functions in flight or on the ground.

4. The ___Load___ control valve is used to meter the amount of bleed air allowed for aircraft systems.

5. A Honeywell GTCP 85 series APU is a self-contained power source that requires only ___fuel___ and ___electricity___ power for operation.

6. The Honeywell GTCP 85 series APU uses a/an ___atomizer___ to inject fuel into the center of the liner, where it is mixed with air and lit by an igniter plug.

7. During operation of an APU, a condition known as ___idle___ exists when the APU operates at full speed and no load is applied.

8. Additional increases in load produces further decreases in shaft r.p.m. called ___droop___.

9. A free-turbine engine has ___no___ mechanical connection between the gas generator turbine and the power turbine.

10. The Rolls-Royce 250 series turboshaft engine's turbine assembly has a/an ___two___ stage gas producer turbine and a/an ___two___ stage power turbine.

Chapter 9
Turboshaft Engines and APUs

MULTIPLE CHOICE QUESTIONS

name:

date:

1. On the GTCP 85 APU the combustion gases flow from the combustion chamber and are collected by the:
   a. Compressor and diffuser
   b. Diffuser and impeller
   c. Torus, which directs the combustion gases into the turbine nozzles ✓
   d. Turbine nozzles

2. The GTCP 85 fuel control system automatically regulates fuel flow to maintain:
   a. Constant engine speed under varying load ✓
   b. Constant fuel pressure
   c. Constant fuel flow
   d. Variable engine speed under varying load

3. For the GTCP 85 APU, engine acceleration (during starting), exhaust temperature and speed are automatically controlled within established limits by:
   a. Controlling fuel pressure
   b. Metering the fuel flow through the fuel control unit ✓
   c. The fuel-air pressure relief valve
   d. Monitoring EGT

4. The four sections of the Rolls-Royce 250 engine are:
   a. Compressor, combustor, turbine, and free turbine
   b. Compressor, fuel control, combustor, and turbine
   c. Compressor, combustor, turbine, and accessory ✓
   d. Accessory, oil tank, turbine, and bearings

5. How many fuel nozzles does the Rolls-Royce 250 have?
   a. 3
   b. 1 ✓
   c. 14
   d. 2

6. The Rolls-Royce 250-C20B model turbine engine has a/an _____ type of compressor.
   a. Single-stage single entry centrifugal compressor
   b. Axial and a centrifugal flow compressor (combination type) ✓
   c. Multistage centrifugal compressor
   d. Multi-axis centrifugal compressor

7. The compressor turbine drives the compressor.
   a. True ✓
   b. False

8. On a Rolls-Royce 250 turbine engine, to gain access to the turbine sections, such as after a hot start, what must be removed?
   a. Fuel control
   b. Combustion section ✓
   c. Compressor inlet guide vanes
   d. Accessory section

9. The lubrication system of the Rolls-Royce 250 engine:
   a. Is a wet sump system
   b. Has one pressure and one scavenge pump ✓
   c. Needs service only when the low-pressure warning illuminates
   d. Has three overboard vents

10. If an operator of a Rolls-Royce 250 engine installed in a helicopter wishes to operate the engine at different N_2 and N_R speeds, the power turbine governor can be reset with:
    a. A ground adjustment prior to flight
    b. Movement of the collective
    c. A beeper switch ✓
    d. Movement of the cyclic

Aircraft Turbine Engines Student Workbook | 57

Chapter 9
Turboshaft Engines and APUs

1. Describe the normal use of the aircraft's APU.

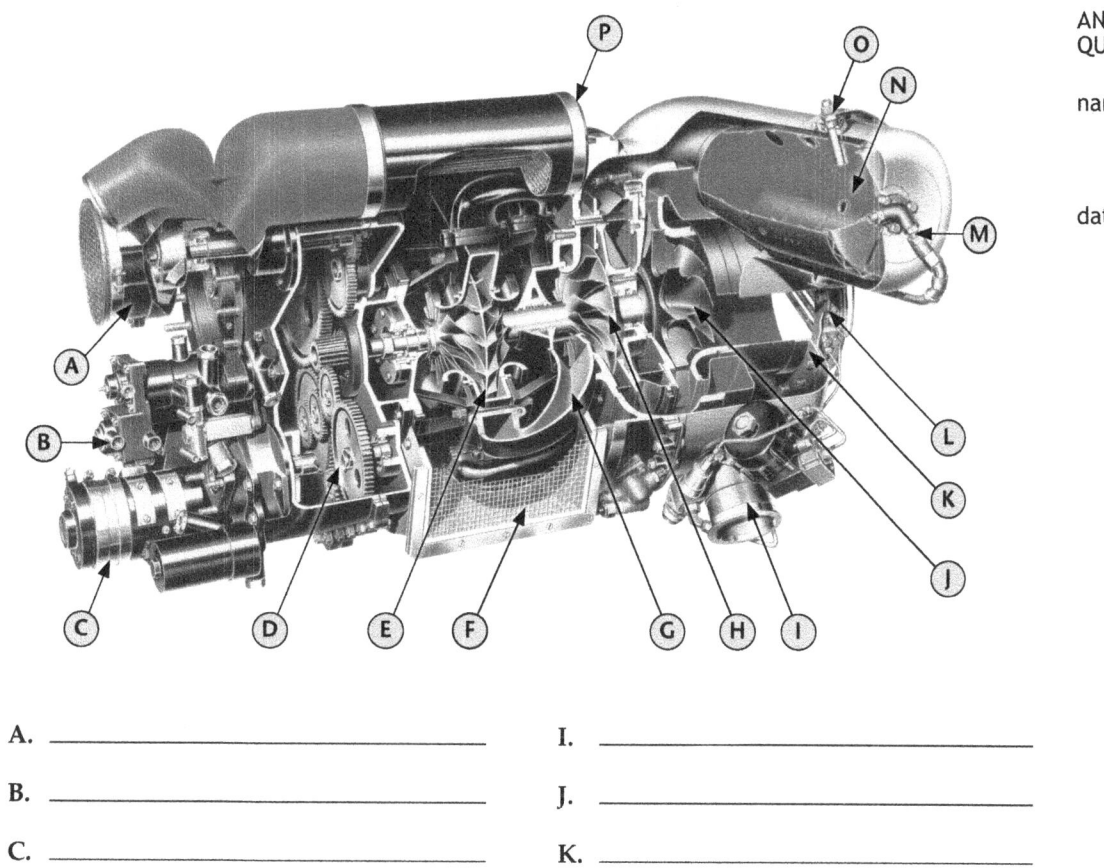

2. Label the components on the cutaway view below.

ANALYSIS QUESTIONS

name:

date:

A. _____

B. _____

C. _____

D. _____

E. _____

F. _____

G. _____

H. _____

I. _____

J. _____

K. _____

L. _____

M. _____

N. _____

O. _____

P. _____

Chapter 9
Turboshaft Engines and APUs

ANALYSIS QUESTIONS

name:

date:

3. Explain the turbine/compressor connections and terminology used to describe these components.

Chapter 10
Inspection and Maintenance

FILL IN THE BLANK QUESTIONS

name:

date:

1. The __on-conditional__ process was assigned to components, on which a determination of continued airworthiness could be made by a/an __visual__ inspection.

2. For engines in normal airline use, a/an __cycle__ is defined as any __flight__ consisting of one takeoff and one landing.

3. Aircraft engines are stressed the most during __start up__ and __take off__ and not during cruise flight conditions.

4. The maximum time an engine can remain installed in an aircraft is limited to a fixed period agreed to by the __aircraft operator__, __engine manufacturer__, and the __airworthiness authority__.

5. Smaller aircraft could be maintained under __14 CFR part 91__ requirements and typically have a/an __progressive__ of inspection schedule.

6. An unscheduled inspection is performed when the engine is subjected to unusual __stress__ or __operating condition__, or exceeds __operating limitations__ or gives unsatisfactory performance/handling.

7. The __borescope__ is an optical device that lets an operator inspect hot section areas of the engine without removing or disassembling the engine.

8. One of the most critical dimensions in the hot section is the __turbine blade tip to case shroud clearance__.

9. For the process of fuel-control trimming, engine r.p.m. is checked against __fuel flow__, __EPR__, and power lever positions.

10. Most hydromechanical fuel controls have adjustments for minimum and maximum __governing speed__, __idle speed__, __acceleration__, and fuel flow.

11. The engine electronic control (EEC) unit can be operated in two modes: normal mode, where engine thrust is set with __EPR__ or alternate mode, where engine thrust is set with __N1__.

12. If the engine's performance is low, a/an __soak solution__ could be used to recover the engine's performance. This is often called a/an __power recovery__ wash.

13. Magnetic particle testing indicates surface or near-surface defects in __ferro-magnetic__.

Chapter 10
Inspection and Maintenance

FILL IN THE BLANK QUESTIONS

name:

date:

14. The fan blades of a turbine engine are susceptible to damage from __foriegn_ __objects__.

15. Turbine blades are subjected to __high temp__ and __high centrifugal force__.

16. Two types of corrosion that are common for turbine engine hot sections are __high temp corrosion__ and __salt erosion__.

17. __false brinring__ occurs when bearings do not rotate for extensive periods.

18. Engine parts are marked permanently or temporarily for __identification__.

19. If the engine is transported by truck, the truck should have an air suspension system to avoid damage to the engine __bearings__.

Chapter 10
Inspection and Maintenance

MULTIPLE CHOICE QUESTIONS

name:

date:

1. What is a cycle?
   a. Any flight consisting of one takeoff and one landing, regardless of length of flight ✓
   b. Any flight consisting of one takeoff and one landing, on very long flights only
   c. The number of operations between overhaul
   d. The length of time between overhaul

2. What are considered to be life-limiting parts on an aircraft engine?
   a. Engine fuel control and fuel nozzles
   b. Compressor and turbine blades
   c. Burner cans and thrust reverser
   d. Compressor and turbine rotating disks ✓

3. Modular maintenance is a type of maintenance that is applicable to:
   a. Older low-bypass turbine engines
   b. Turbojet engines
   c. Modern high-bypass turbofan engines ✓
   d. All the above

4. What type of maintenance scheduling is used by major air carriers?
   a. Line maintenance and overhaul checks
   b. Line checks and A, B, C, and D checks ✓
   c. 100 hours and annual inspection
   d. Progressive type of inspection

5. What is the most extensive maintenance check used by commercial air carriers?
   a. A check
   b. B check
   c. C check
   d. D check ✓

6. Which is not a cause for an unscheduled inspection?
   a. Engine reaches maximum number of operating cycles ✓
   b. Performance deterioration
   c. Bird strike
   d. Overspeed

7. What type of equipment is used to look into the engine for FOD without removing or disassembling the engine?
   a. Borescope ✓
   b. Inspection mirror
   c. Ultrasonic diagnostic equipment
   d. X-ray equipment

8. Over many hours of operation, turbine engine EGT will typically _____, relative to a specified EPR or torque value.
   a. Decrease
   b. Increase ✓
   c. Remain constant
   d. Fluctuate

9. What is not a reason for fuel control trimming?
   a. Fuel control replacement
   b. Flight crew reports that engine parameters are not within limits
   c. Engine performance check reveals that engine parameters are not within limits
   d. Fuel filter replacement ✓

10. What adjustments can a technician make to a fuel metering unit if the engine is equipped with an engine electronic control unit?
    a. Governing speeds
    b. Idle speed
    c. Maximum EGT
    d. No adjustments can be made ✓

Chapter 10
Inspection and Maintenance

MULTIPLE CHOICE QUESTIONS

name:

date:

11. What type of maintenance is often performed if aircraft engines are operated in dirty, dusty, or corrosive environments?
    a. Hot section inspection
    b. Line inspection
    c. Compressor and turbine wash
    d. Oil change

12. Which of the following methods is not a nondestructive testing method?
    a. Magnetic particle
    b. Eddy current
    c. Tensile testing
    d. Ultrasonic

13. Magnetic particle inspection is used with what type of metal?
    a. Plastics
    b. Steel
    c. Aluminum
    d. Magnesium

14. Fan blade fatigue failure is caused by:
    a. Foreign object damage (FOD)
    b. Heat
    c. High centrifugal forces and resonant vibration
    d. Corrosion

15. Turbine engine blades will _____ in length during engine operation.
    a. Decrease
    b. Increase
    c. Vary
    d. Both b and c are correct

16. Turbine blades getting longer is called what?
    a. Creep
    b. Tensile stress
    c. Growth dimension
    d. Blade extension

17. What is a type of corrosion that is common for turbine engine hot sections?
    a. Sulfidation
    b. Exfoliation
    c. Stress
    d. Galvanic

18. What is the most common cause of damage to ball bearings?
    a. Dirt or foreign matter
    b. Misalignment
    c. Overload
    d. High temperature

19. Approved methods for marking parts are:
    a. Electrolytic etch, metal stamping, vibration peening and electric arc scribing
    b. Electrolytic etch, soapstone, metal stamping, and vibration peening
    c. Electrolytic etch, metal stamping, vibration peening, or engraving methods
    d. Soapstone, acid etching, and electric arc scribing

20. Lead or metallic pencils may not be used to mark parts because they can:
    a. Result in carburization
    b. Result in intergranular attack
    c. Leave permanent markings on the parts
    d. Both a and b are correct

Chapter 10
Inspection and Maintenance

ANALYSIS QUESTIONS

name:

date:

1. Explain the differences between operating cycles and time between overhaul.

2. Discuss the advantages of modular turbine design.

3. Discuss the advantages of using a borescope or similar device for engine hot section inspections.

4. Describe what procedures must be followed when an engine performance check must be performed.

5. Describe the function of the data entry plug on engines equipped with an engine electronic control (EEC) unit.

Chapter 10
Inspection and Maintenance

ANALYSIS QUESTIONS

name:

date:

6. What information is stored in the data entry plug?

7. Explain a typical engine compressor wash procedure.

8. Describe what procedures to follow to determine if a component or part is made of steel or aluminum.

9. Describe compressor blade damage and discuss typical critical areas.

Aircraft Turbine Engines Student Workbook | 65

Chapter 11
Fault Analysis

FILL IN THE BLANK QUESTIONS

name:

date:

1. Gas turbine engine maintenance practices frequently include ___inflight insite performance___ as a means of detecting mechanical deterioration.

2. ___built in test equipment___ records EGT information, spool speeds, fuel flow, EPR, and other engine design parameters.

3. Engine sensors supply data through the ___electronic engine control___ to the engine diagnostic system.

4. Modern transport category aircraft are usually equipped with an onboard ___fault___ ___detection system___ that can display and communicate with the ___Bite___.

5. Most of the vibrations in large turbine engines are generated by the ___fan___ and the ___compressor rotor___.

6. The accelerometers send signals that are ___proportional___ to the engine vibration.

7. The ___onsite balancing system___ lets you select which balance weights to change on the engine to decrease engine vibration.

8. Typically, advances in engine performance hinge on a new engine's ability to operate at ___higher___ temperatures.

9. Nickel-based superalloys possess ___high strength___ and ___toughness___ at high temperatures.

10. The ceramic coating used on some turbine blades provides a/an ___thermal barrier___ between the superalloy and the hot combustion gas.

Chapter 11
Fault Analysis

MULTIPLE CHOICE QUESTIONS

name:

date:

1. The engine condition trend monitoring system uses the following parameters:
   a. Pressure altitude (PA), outside air temperature (OAT), turbine inlet temperature (TIT), and compressor speed
   b. Pressure altitude (PA), outside air temperature (OAT), turbine inlet temperature (TIT), and turbine speed
   c. Burner can pressure, outside air temperature, and pressure altitude
   d. Burner can pressure, turbine speed, turbine inlet temperature (TIT), and outside air temperature (OAT)

   Answer: a

2. Which of these malfunctions can be detected with an onboard diagnostic system?
   a. Oil leaks
   b. Cracks in air ducts
   c. High EGT
   d. Foreign object damage (FOD)

   Answer: c

3. What is the function of the fault detection systems on modern aircraft?
   a. Display and communicate with the built-in test equipment (BITE)
   b. Initiate tests from the multipurpose control display (MCDU)
   c. Correct engine malfunctions
   d. Both a and b are correct

   Answer: d

4. The airborne vibration monitoring system consists of the following three components:
   a. Accelerometer, remote charge converter, and the signal conditioner unit
   b. Accelerometer, remote charge converter, and signal amplifier
   c. Data collector, remote charge converter, and signal amplifier
   d. Signal amplifier, accelerometer, and signal conditioner unit

   Answer: a

5. What is the function of the engine balancing system (EBS)?
   a. Select balance weights to decrease engine vibration
   b. Automatically adds balance weight to decrease engine vibration.
   c. Inform the flight crew to shut down the engine if engine vibration exceeds limits
   d. Automatically shuts down engine if engine vibration exceeds limits.

   Answer: a

6. What material is often used for the turbine blades in modern engines?
   a. Aluminum
   b. Stainless steel
   c. Nickel-based superalloys
   d. Titanium

   Answer: c

7. What material is often used for the fan blades in modern engines?
   a. Aluminum
   b. Stainless steel
   c. Nickel-based superalloys
   d. Titanium

   Answer: d

8. What is the function of metallic coatings such as chromium?
   a. Provide thermal barrier
   b. Provide corrosion and oxidation protection
   c. Allow higher engine TIT
   d. None of the above

   Answer: b

9. What is the function of thermal barrier coatings?
   a. Allow decreased engine TIT
   b. Provide corrosion and oxidation protection
   c. Provide a thermal barrier between superalloy and combustion gases
   d. None of the above

   Answer: c

10. What is the purpose of a Spectrographic Oil Analysis Program (SOAP)?
    a. To detect the quality of the lubrication oil
    b. To detect abnormal wear of the engine or gearbox
    c. To alert the flight crew of an engine lubrication problem
    d. Used by maintenance personnel to determine oil change intervals

    Answer: b

11. The minimum equipment list (MEL) is intended to permit an aircraft:
    a. To operate with inoperative items of equipment for a period until repairs can be made
    b. To operate with inoperative items indefinitely
    c. There is no such thing as a MEL
    d. Not operate unless very component is operational

    Answer: a

Chapter 11
Fault Analysis

ANALYSIS QUESTIONS

name:

date:

1. List the types of sensors that are used for real-time monitoring.

2. Explain why onboard diagnostic systems will not detect cracks, oil leaks, or foreign object damage (FOD).

3. Explain the operation of the airborne vibration monitoring (AVM) system.

4. Explain the operation of the engine balancing system (EBS).

5. Why are titanium fan blades used for the cold section of the engine, and nickel-based superalloys and some ceramics for the hot section of the engine?

Chapter 11
Fault Analysis

ANALYSIS QUESTIONS

name:

date:

6. Explain the difference between metallic coatings such as chromium and the thermal barrier coating used on turbine blades.

7. Discuss the advantages of a spectrographic oil analysis program (SOAP).

8. Why is SOAP ineffective if the samples are not taken from the same location?

9. What is the purpose of the Rolls-Royce engine health management (EHM)?

Chapter 12
Turbine Engine Manufacturing

FILL IN THE BLANK QUESTIONS

name:

date:

1. Sand casting is a technique usually used for _low production volume_ processes.
2. High-pressure casting is usually used for _high production_ processes.
3. Single crystal turbine blades are produced from high temperature nickel alloy that are cast by _investment casting_.
4. _Forging_ is the plastic deformation of metals into desired shapes by compression with or without a die.
5. The shielding gas used with gas metal arc welding (GMAW) is either _helium_ or _argon_.
6. _Friction stir_ welding uses frictional heat generated by a rotating spindle.
7. Electro-chemical machining is used for _etching_.
8. _Chemical milling_ is the process of removing large amounts of metal by means of chemical etching.
9. Most aerospace alloys like aluminum, titanium, and steel can be _softening_ _heat treated_ or _annealed_ by heat treating processes.
10. The _autoclave_ is the principal equipment for producing high-quality composite parts.

Chapter 12
Turbine Engine Manufacturing

MULTIPLE CHOICE QUESTIONS

name:

date:

1. Which is true of sand casting?
   a. Several types of materials are used to make sand molds ✓
   b. It is used for high-production volume processes
   c. It is used for low-quality processes
   d. The molds can be reused multiple times

2. What type of material is used to make die castings?
   a. Sand
   b. Copper or brass
   c. Cast iron or steel ✓
   d. Clay

3. What type of casting technique uses wax to make a pattern?
   a. Sand casting
   b. Die casting
   c. Investment casting ✓
   d. Forging

4. What technique uses compression and dies to shape metals?
   a. Sand casting
   b. Die casting
   c. Forging ✓
   d. CNC machining

5. What type of shielding gas is used for gas tungsten arc welding (GTAW)?
   a. Helium
   b. Argon
   c. Oxygen
   d. Both a and b are correct ✓

6. What type of welding process uses a non-consumable electrode?
   a. Gas metal arc welding (GMAW)
   b. Gas tungsten arc welding (GTAW) ✓
   c. Spot welding
   d. Plasma arc welding

7. What type of machining process is used for etching or to create unstressed, high precision parts?
   a. Electro-chemical machining ✓
   b. Electro-discharge machining
   c. Chemical milling
   d. Laser welding

8. What type of machining process is used for creating shapes within components and assemblies?
   a. Electro-chemical machining
   b. Electro-discharge machining ✓
   c. Chemical milling
   d. Laser welding

9. Solution heat treatment will make the metal:
   a. Softer
   b. Stronger ✓
   c. Less brittle
   d. More ductile

10. Why are metal bolts and parts often cadmium plated?
    a. To increase wear resistance
    b. To increase heat resistance
    c. To provide an anti-seize surface
    d. To increase corrosion resistance ✓

Aircraft Turbine Engines Student Workbook | 73

Chapter 12
Turbine Engine Manufacturing

ANALYSIS QUESTIONS

name:

date:

1. Compare the different types of casting techniques and discuss the advantages and disadvantages of each.

2. Explain the differences between gas metal arc welding and gas tungsten arc welding.

3. Compare and contrast electro-chemical machining, electro-discharge machining, and chemical milling.

4. Explain the process of **solution heat treatment**.

5. Why do we anneal and heat treat metals?

Chapter 12
Turbine Engine Manufacturing

ANALYSIS QUESTIONS

name:

date:

6. Explain the principle of electroplating.